Mortuus Vindictae

(DEAD REVENGE)

By William Armstrong

FADE IN

INT. STEVENSON MANOR PROPERTY - CEMETARY - NIGHT

The camera sweeps across the STEVENSON MANSION GROUNDS. Trees are ruffled by a soft, autumn breeze. Leaves tumble down a driveway leading to the HOUSE. We hear the sound of distant arguing. The sweep continues through the cemetery on the property, settling on a couple. They are EDWARD and JEANNIE IRVINE. The couple lies on a blanket, trying to UNDRESS for SEX.

                    EDWARD
          Lie still. I've almost got it.

                    JEANNIE
          You're worse at this now than when
          we were in high school.

                    EDWARD
          Your bra was easier to open in high
          school. Hold still.

                    JEANNIE
          You definitely had more practice.
          Wait a minute. Let me help you.

                    EDWARD
          Damn! It's colder tonight that I
          thought it would be.

                    JEANNIE
          Did you think my nipples looked like that
          because you touched them? Go get another
          blanket from the car.

                    EDWARD
          If we just get started, we'll warm up and
          be fine. Damn, it's creepy as hell out
          here.

                    JEANNIE
          Forget the bra. Help me out of my pants.

                    EDWARD
          Alright. Goddammit. I don't believe it. I
          can't unsnap your pants either.

                    JEANNIE
          Are you kidding? Oh, for god's sake, stop!
          This is ridiculous. Just stop.

They start to redress themselves. Both are in a
huff and sullen. The camera pans the distance,
settling on Edward and Jeannie, finished
dressing.

                    EDWARD
     There you go again. Every time I want to
     have some fun, you kill it.

                    JEANNIE
     Don't blame me. You let the tour group
     leave without us.

                    EDWARD
     This was the last house on the tour. They
     were leaving anyway.

                    JEANNIE
     And it was fun, up to this point. You know
     I love haunted house tours. This was just
     stupid. I mean, what's the point?

                    EDWARD
     To maybe put some excitement into our
     marriage. To try something different; a
     little wrong. Let's calm down. Relax for a
     few minutes. We can try again.

                    JEANNIE
     Let's just Go home. It's obviously been
     too long. I'm over it. Let's go home. I
     could use a hot drink.

                    EDWARD
     At least I'm trying something to put some
     spark into our marriage.

                    JEANNIE
     And I appreciate it, sweetheart. I'm just
     not in the mood.

                    EDWARD
     Fine. Why don't we at least go look at the
     mansion before we leave.

The camera cuts to a shot of the STEVENSON MANSION. It is old,
decaying, in the architectural style of a GOTHIC southern plantation
home.

                              JEANNIE
          Alright.

                              EDWARD
          Wait. Listen

Both fall silent.

                              JEANNIE
          I don't…

                              EDWARD
          Look out!

EDWARD grabs JEANNIE and pulls her out of the way. Both fall to the
ground. The camera snaps to the SPOT where they stood. There is the
sound of THUDDING IMPACT. The camera moves slowly to a shallow IMPACT
CRATER. Edward and Jeannie are covered in dirt and grass.

                              EDWARD
          What the hell!

The camera shows an OBJECT embedded in the impact crater. It is a
HEADSTONE.

                              JEANNIE
          Look at the name.

We see the name on the headstone. It reads ALYSSA CARLA STEVENSON. We
see EDWARD'S look of horror.

                              EDWARD
          Oh, my god.

The scene fades to the OPENING CREDITS. Overlaying the credits are
monochrome photographs of a COUPLE. Both are in WEDDING ATTIRE. They
are JACOB and ALYSSA STEVENSON. The man is stern and serious. The
woman is young and smiling.

The photograph changes to other photographs, showing a PROGRESSION
through their life. Each photograph shows them aging. The man remains
STERN and SERIOUS. The woman ages badly. Her smile is absent and her
face becomes CARE-WORN and DESPAIRING. The photographs then show the
man standing beside ANOTHER smiling, young woman. Both are in wedding
attire. The credits end.

INT. HELEN AND JASON IRVINE'S HOUSE - DINING ROOM - NIGHT

Edward, Jeannie, JASON (Edward's brother) and HELEN (Jason's wife) sit
around the dining room table. The remnants of dinner cover the table.
They pick at leftovers and sip wine.

                         HELEN
So, a headstone almost killed you?

                         JEANNIE
Stupid, right?

                         EDWARD
How can you shrug it off? You were there.
You saw it.

                         JEANNIE
I know, sweetheart. And it scared the hell
out of me. I'm just saying, it had to be a
prank. Some kids trying ruin our evening.

                         EDWARD
Yeah, some kids.

                         JEANNIE
Please don't start.

                         EDWARD
It wasn't some kids. It was…something
else.

                         JASON
What do you think it was?

                         EDWARD
I don't know. I think it's strange that it
happened at that exact moment, in that
exact place.

                         HELEN
What were you two doing there in the first
place?

                         JEANNIE
Fooling around, and not doing a very good
of it.

                         EDWARD
We were trying to have some fun.
Remembering what life was like before kids
and work and a mortgage and being boring
adults.

                         JEANNIE
It's been a while for us that we've had an
adventure. Plus, a graveyard on a dark,
windy night isn't exactly conducive to an
hour of passion for me.

                         JASON
Nothing wrong with a little night time
fun. In a cemetery? That sounds awesome.
Not much chance of someone interrupting
you.

                         HELEN
Okay, so what happened.

                         EDWARD
Nothing. We tried to mess around, got
upset and decided to call it a night.
Then, we were almost killed.

                         JEANNIE
Ed, relax. It was strange. We can't
explain it. We got dressed and decided to
check out the mansion. It was a favorite
pick on a list of Halloween hot spots in
the city.

                         JASON
I love those.

                         HELEN
Me, too.

                         JEANNIE
It was fun. Then we stopped for dinner as
a group. After that, we all drove to the
Stevenson Mansion. You know it, don't you?
On the north side of town?

                         HELEN
It's a rundown, old place.

                         JASON
But really cool. A lot of creepy stories
about it, from back in the day.

                         HELEN
I didn't know it was supposed to be
haunted.

                         JEANNIE
Yeah. Some bizarre, unproven stuff is
supposed to have happened.

                    EDWARD
But, it didn't the night we were there.
All that happened was, a headstone ruined
our evening.

                    JEANNIE
No, sweetheart. Trying to have sex in a
public place ruined our evening. We're not
twenty years old anymore.

                    JASON
What time did it happen?

                    EDWARD
A little after midnight.

                    JASON
And you were on the Stevenson property?

                    EDWARD
Yes, about a hundred yards from the
mansion.

                    JASON
Hmm.

Everyone stares at Jason in silence.

                    HELEN
What are you thinking?

                    JASON
I don't know. The Stevenson Mansion was
built in the eighteen hundreds. No-one
knows much about it. I looked it up after
you called us, and there isn't a lot.
(Jason falls silent.)

                    EDWARD
                (After a beat.)
And? So?

                    JASON
What I could find is…frightening.

                    JEANNIE
Like what? What did you find?

                    JASON
The owner of the house, Jacob Stevenson,
was a bastard.

                              Edward
You mean, he had no parents?

                              HELEN
You're thinking of an orphan.

                              JEANNIE
He was an orphan?

                              JASON
                         (Laughing.)
No. I mean he was cruel, malicious. A
bastard. He was supposed to have killed
several women. One of them was his first
wife.

                              EDWARD
My god.

                              JEANNIE
You're kidding?

                              HELEN
How many women?

                              JASON
No-one knows for sure. He hid his crimes
well, apparently. But, it's a theory, just
a guess, that he killed eleven women.

                              EDWARD
Unbelievable.

                              JEANNIE
That son of a bitch.

                              HELEN
And, nothing came of it? They had to have
conducted investigations.

                              JASON
It was a different time. Women were second
class citizens. Not revered, like they are
today.

                              HELEN
                         (Smiling.)
You're awesome.

                              EDWARD
Yeah, nice. So, what else?

                         JEANNIE
          (To Edward.) Always so romantic.

                         JASON
                       (Interrupting.)
          Anyway…with Jacob's reputation as a great
          businessman, he had influence in the city.
          He probably paid for silence. And, the
          deaths were never really looked into.
          Then, he married. He wanted a son to pass
          his legacy on to.

                         JEANNIE
                        (Angry.)
          Some legacy.

                         HELEN
          Relax. (To Jason.) Go on, babe.

                         JASON
          He didn't treat her well. There were
          rumors of physical and mental abuse,
          cheating and children by other women.
          Then, she disappeared, without a trace.
          Within only a few months, he had
          remarried. He was supposed to have treated
          his second wife just as badly. She went
          missing also. Then, he died, leaving
          everything to his son by his second wife.

                         EDWARD
          Wait a minute. The first wife. What was
          her name?

                         JASON
          Alyssa. Alyssa Carla Stevenson.

                         EDWARD
          Damn!

                         JEANNIE
          My god.

                         HELEN
          Why? What's wrong?

Close up on Edward.

                         EDWARD
          That was the name on the headstone that
          almost killed us.

INT. JASON AND HELEN'S HOUSE - DEN - A FEW MINUTES LATER

Edward and Jason are sitting in the DEN, in front of a COMPUTER. The
den is CLUTTERED and MESSY. Jason types, while the two men talk.

                    EDWARD
          So, what are we doing?

                    JASON
          I wanted to show you what I found on the
          Stevensons. Like I said, the old man had a
          son by wife number two. The wife's name
          was…Lydia. He was fifty-three and she was
          twenty-two when they married.

                    EDWARD
          Robbing the cradle, huh?

                    JASON
          I guess so. Anyway, the son's name
          was…you're not going to believe this. His
          name was Edward.

                    EDWARD
          You're kidding. (He looks at the computer
          screen.) You're not kidding. What was the
          son's middle name?

                    JASON
          Umm…Andrew.

                    EDWARD
                    (Shocked.)
          Now you really are joking around.
          Seriously, what was it?

                    JASON
          I'm being serious, bro. Look at this. I
          found his birth records online.

                    EDWARD
          I don't believe it. (He HURRIES from the
          room.)

                    JASON
          It's a coincidence, Ed. Where are you
          going?

INT. JASON AND HELEN'S HOME - LIVING ROOM - A FEW MINUTES LATER

Jeannie and Helen sit in the living room watching TELEVISION. Edward
hurries into the room and grabs his JACKET. Jason stops in the living
room.

                    EDWARD
          I'm leaving. Helen or Jason can drive you
          home, if you want to stay.

He then EXITS the FRONT DOOR.

                    JEANNIE
          Ed? What's wrong? Why are you leaving?

                    HELEN
          Jason, what's wrong? Why is he so upset?

                    JASON
          We found something online.

                    JEANNIE
          Ed! Wait!

She grabs her JACKET, and then EXITS the front
door.

INT. EDWARD'S CAR - A FEW MINUTES LATER

Edward and Jeannie SPEED through the night in Edward's CAR. Jeannie is
FRANTIC and Edward is clearly DISTRAUGHT.

          Ed, please slow down. You blew through
          that stop sign back there! (Edward remains
          silent.) Please, sweetheart, just tell
          what happened. Did Jason say something
          that upset you?

                    EDWARD
          No.

                    JEANNIE
          Then why did you leave in such a hurry?

Edward SLOWS down the CAR.

                    EDWARD
          Jason was researching the Stevenson's
          family history. He had found some
          information about Jacob's son.

                    JEANNIE
          Okay. So what did he find?

                    EDWARD
        The son's first name was Edward.

                    JEANNIE
                 (Smiling.)
        Oh. Well, it's a coincidence. Edward is a
        popular name. It's really no reason for
        you to be upset.

                    EDWARD
        That's not why I'm upset.

                    JEANNIE
        Then what is it?

                    EDWARD
        His middle name was Andrew.

                    JEANNIE
                 (Her smile fades.)
        My god. Still, sweetheart, it has to be a
        coincidence.

                    EDWARD
        I know that. A laughable, one-in-a-billion
        chance.

                    JEANNIE
        I don't understand. What else did you
        find?

                    EDWARD
        His mother, Stevenson's second wife- her
        first name was Lydia.

Jeannie stares HORRIFIED.

                    JEANNIE
        That's your mother's name.

Edward pulls the car into the DRIVEWAY of their home and SHUTS OFF the
engine.

                    EDWARD
        And, listen to this. The son's birth date is August 2nd. The
        same as mine.

Edward EXITs the car. Jeannie sits for a moment, processing the
INFORMATION.

INT. EDWARD AND JEANNIES HOME - BEDROOM - A FEW MINUTES LATER

Edward is RUMMAGING through dresser drawers, PULLING out a LONG-SLEEVED SHIRT and BLACK SOCKS. He MOVES to the closet and takes out BLACK PANTS and BLACK SHOES. From a box on a shelf in the closet, He retrieves a BLACK, KNIT CAP.)

                    JEANNIE
          Ed! Edward! Where are you going?

                    EDWARD
          Back to the mansion. I need to get in and
          look around. Do we have a flashlight?

                    JEANNIE
          Ed, you can't break into that house. I
          don't feel like bailing you out of jail.
          Now, just stop, calm down and think.

                    EDWARD
          Jeannie, if I stop to think about it, I
          won't want to go.

                    JEANNIE
          Anything in that house that could have
          answered any questions you have would have
          been removed or stolen years ago. Places
          like that lie abandoned for years. They
          get broken into. They get vandalized.
          There won't be anything left.

Edward SITS on the bed, dejected.

                    JEANNIE (CONT.)
          There's got to be somewhere else we can
          get the answers you need.

                    EDWARD
          Damn it. You're right.

                    JEANNIE
          The first two places we can look are the
          library and the hall of records.

                    EDWARD
          You're right, of course. Wait, you said
          'we'.

                    JEANNIE
          I want to go with you. I have questions of
          my own. We'll go first thing in the
          morning. (She leans forward and KISSES
          Edward.) Come on, sweetheart. Let's finish

                    what we started last night in the
                    graveyard.

The scene fades to black.

INT. EDWARD AND JEANNIE'S BEDROOM - 2 A.M. THE NEXT MORNING

Edward and Jeannie are ASLEEP in bed. Jeannie is STARTLED awake by a
NOISE from the ATTIC.

                              JEANNIE
                    Edward. Ed. Wake up!

Edward continues to sleep.

                              JEANNIE (Cont.)
                    Goddammit!

She gets out of bed and moves to the Bedroom door. She opens it and
peers out into the DARK HALLWAY. Another sound from the attic startles
her. She shuts the door and HURRIES to Edward who is still asleep. She
SHAKES him.

                              JEANNIE (cont.)
                    Edward! Wake up, Ed!

Edward wakes up, pushing her away.

                              EDWARD
                    I'm awake. What?

                              JEANNIE
                    I heard someone moving around in the attic.

                              EDWARD
                    What?

                              JEANNIE
                    I clearly heard someone moving around the attic.

Both REACT to another sound from above them.

                              EDWARD
                    You're right. Grab your phone and call 911.

Jeannie retrieves her TELEPHONE and speaks into it. Edward Gets a GUN
from the closet. They move to the door and open it. They peer into the
dark hallway.

INT. EDWARD AND JEANNIE'S HOUSE - SECOND FLOOR LANDING - A FEW MINUTES
LATER

                              JEANNIE
          I told 911 we have an intruder. They're
          sending someone.

                              EDWARD
          Not fast enough. Stay here.

Edward moves down the hallway. In the CEILING, we see a pull-cord for
the attic PULL-DOWN STAIRWAY. Edward pulls the cord and the attic
stairs descend. He climbs them and shines the FLASHLIGHT around the
attic, showing us that it is empty. He descends the stairs.

                              EDWARD
          Nothing. Where are the police?

                              JEANNIE
          We just called them. Maybe we should wait
          for the police outside.

                              EDWARD
          No, this is our home. I'm checking it out.

                              JEANNIE
                         (Sarcastic.)
          My macho man.

INT. EDWARD AND JEANNIE'S HOUSE - SECOND FLOOR LANDING - A FEW MINUTES
LATER

Edward and Jeannie hear a SOUND coming from Jeannie's ART STUDIO. They
tip toe to the studio door. Edward quickly opens the door and flips on
a light switch. The studio is empty. They are startled by a NOISE on
the FIRST FLOOR of the house.

INT. EDWARD AND JEANNIE'S HOME - STAIRWAY - A FEW MINUTES LATER

They tiptoe downstairs, hearing only RUSTLINGS from the living room.
They reach the FIRST FLOOR. Jeannie looks around a corner and RECOILS.

INT. EDWARD AND JEANNIE'S HOME - FIRST FLOOR - A FEW MINUTES LATER

Jeannie grabs Edward's arm and points towards a living room window. We
clearly see the DARK, MOVING FIGURE of a woman. Edward raises the gun,
pointing it in the direction of the figure. As he COCKS THE TRIGGER,
with his other hand, he flips on a light switch. We see the living
room is empty.

They are startled by a loud knock on the FRONT DOOR of the house.

                              JEANNIE
          That must be the police. Give me the gun.
          I'll put it away in the kitchen.

                              EDWARD
             Alright. Turn on some lights also.

As Jeannie disappears into the kitchen, Edward opens the front door,
turning on the PORCH LIGHT. Two POLICE OFFICERS are at the door.

                              POLICEMAN
             You called the police?

INT. THE CITY HALL OF RECORDS - COMPUTER ROOM - DAY

Edward and Jeannie sit in the CITY HALL OF RECORDS, In front of a
computer.

                              JEANNIE
             What, exactly, are we looking for?

                              EDWARD
             I want to find more information about
             Jacob Stevenson's son, Edward. And, while
             we're at it, find out what we can about
             his mother, Lydia.

                              JEANNIE
             I have some questions myself. The first
             wife, Alyssa, did she have any children?
             And, are there any living descendants of
             Edward? Who did he marry? What was her
             maiden name? I'll log onto the computer
             next to you.

Jeannie logs onto the COMPUTER and starts to
type.

                              EDWARD
             Okay. So…Lydia. Who was she? Here she is.
             Her maiden name was Del fuego. No
             information on her family.

                              JEANNIE
             But, according to census records, Lydia
             Del fuego was…interesting. A servant in
             the mansion.

                              EDWARD
             A servant, huh?

                              JEANNIE
             Uh, huh. And, listen to this. It's
             recorded that there was a baby girl born
             to the first wife, Alyssa. No father

listed. But, in the next census, four
years later, the child's name doesn't
appear. (She looks at Edward.) Oh, my god.

                    EDWARD
Let's not jump to conclusions. The child
may have died from natural causes. People
were still dying from the flu in those
days.

                    JEANNIE
But, who's to say Jacob wasn't the father?
And, if he wanted a son…

                    EDWARD
I wouldn't have put it past him, with
everything else we've heard about him.

                    JEANNIE
And, it would have left the path to
inheritance open for the first born son.
The more I hear about the old man, the
more I hate him.

                    EDWARD
Listen to this. Alyssa is noted as having
born a daughter. Her name was June. She
appears in the family records until Alyssa
disappears, then her name is gone too.

                    JEANNIE
I'm going to search the newspapers during
that time.

Both stare at their computer screens for a few
seconds.

                EDWARD/JEANNIE
Oh, my god.

                    JEANNIE
Within a year of their disappearance,
people began to avoid the house. There
were rumors of unexplained occurrences
connected with the mansion, and the
family.

                    EDWARD
It says here, there was a library,
separate from the house. The son went to
the police, and by the time they entered
the library, they found a terrible scene.

There was blood and books of hoodoo. But,
they never found Jacob. His second wife
had gone missing, also.

                    JEANNIE
          I wonder if there's a layout of the
          mansion and grounds we could look at?

                    EDWARD
          Let's find out.

Fade to black, as they stand.

INT. CITY HALL OF RECORDS - A FEW MINUTES LATER - DAY

Jeannie and Edward stare at an OLD MAP detailing the STEVENSON MANSION
and surrounding grounds.

                    EDWARD
          That was smart, telling them we were
          doing research for the historical
          society.

                    JEANNIE
          It was sort of true. Anything we
          find out, we can let the society
          know.

                    EDWARD
          Here it is. According to the map
          legend, this symbol shows where the
          house library was built.

                    JEANNIE
          To the west of the house.

                    EDWARD
          Why would they even need it? Here,
          it shows a large study next to the
          master bedroom. Did the newspapers
          mention what kind of books the
          Stevenson's kept?

                    JEANNIE
          No. Why? What are you thinking?

                    EDWARD
          Well, you said were stories of
          strange things connected to the
          house.

                    JEANNIE

And with the family. Wait, are you
thinking witchcraft or voodoo?

                    EDWARD
No. Jacob doesn't seem the type.

                    JEANNIE
What about the second wife? If she
can get rid of the old man, she and
her son get everything.

                    EDWARD
You know I don't believe in ghosts.

                    JEANNIE
We need to keep an open mind, sweetheart.

                    EDWARD
    Alright, let's go.

As they begin to leave, an ELDERLY WOMAN approaches them. She is ETTA
JAMES, one of the city's record keepers.

                    ETTA
Excuse me. Were you talking about
the Stevenson house?

                    EDWARD
Yes, we were.

                    ETTA
I heard you mention Lydia Stevenson,
is that correct?

                    JEANNIE
Yes, we did.

                    ETTA
You were right about the family
having problems. Strange things
happened throughout that second
marriage.

                    JEANNIE
Like what?

                    ETTA
Noises. Strange lights. Screams. In
other words, ghosts.

                              EDWARD
                         (Sarcastic.)
          Really? Well, we have to go now.

                              JEANNIE
          Edward, relax. (To Etta.) And Lydia
          caused these things? How?

                              ETTA
          Oh, no, dear. It wasn't Lydia. It
          was the first wife, Alyssa.

                              JEANNIE
          So, she was still living in the
          house during the second marriage?

                              ETTA
          I didn't say she was living.

The scene fades to black as Etta walks away.

EXT. SERENA STEVENSON'S HOUSE- DAY

Jeannie and Edward knock on the door of SERENA STEVENSON'S house.
SERENA opens the door. She is in her early thirties, but looks older.
She looks tired, haggard. She has dark circles under her eyes. Her
hair is stringy with copious strands of grey, despite her young age.
Her hands tremble.

                              SERENA
          Hello. Mr. and Mrs. Irvine?

                              JEANNNIE
          Yes. Miss Stevenson?

                              SERENA
          That's right. Come on in.

                              JEANNIE
          Thank you.

They follow Serena into her KITCHEN and sit at the kitchen table.

                              SERENA
          Can I get you some coffee? I have instant.

                              JEANNIE
          No, thank you. I'm sorry for saying
          so, but you don't look like you're
          feeling very well.

                    SERENA
I'm not. I haven't gotten a full
night's sleep in years.

                    JEANNIE
Have you seen a doctor?

                    Serena
A psychiatrist. But it didn't do any good. Damn Alyssa.

                    EDWARD
Why do you say that?

                    SERENA
My family's cursed. You said on the
phone you know our family's history.

                    EDWARD
That's why we're here.

                    JEANNIE
What were saying about Alyssa?

                    SERENA
Her husband, Jacob, murdered her.
Ever since, she's plagued my family,
going all the way back to Lydia.
Every damn night. I hear sounds,
voices, footsteps. Every generation
of our family has been harassed by
Alyssa.

                    EDWARD
Do you know why?

                    SERENA
Because her own daughter was passed
over for the inheritance. Alyssa
never forgave our family. Everything
June got, she got because she
married Edward.

                    JEANNIE
Wait. June lived? And, she married
Edward, Lydia's son?

                    EDWARD
Weren't they half-siblings?

                    SERENA
Yes. My family's messed up. It all
started with Jacob. And now, we all

live in fear. I guess it's Alyssa's
revenge.

SERENA lights a CIGARETTE.

                    EDWARD
          Have you thought about moving?

                    SERENA
          I've moved several times in my life.
          No matter where I live, it's always
          the same. Last night, from midnight
          until sunup, doors throughout the
          house opened and slammed shut. My
          husband left, and my two boys say
          they are haunted too. God, I hate
          that word.

                    JEANNIE
          Does she ever physically assault you?

                    SERENA
          Sometimes. Mostly, she's just wearing me out.

                    EDWARD
          Sleeping Pills?

                    SERENA
          I tried those once. I woke up the
          first night, on the second floor
          landing, with a bathrobe cord around
          my neck, and the other tied to the
          banister. I won't use them again.

                    JEANNIE
          What about having a priest bless your home?

                    SERENA
          I tried. He stayed about ten
          minutes, then fled when things
          started to move on their own.

                    EDWARD
          It sounds like Alyssa's nothing more
          than a poltergeist.

                    SERENA
          Normally, I'd agree with you. But,
          it's more than that. I mentioned she
          drove my husband away. That's not
          all of it. Any pets I've ever owned

have either run away or she's killed
them. You don't want to know how.

                    JEANNIE
God, I'm sorry.

                    EDWARD
You're sure it's Alyssa?

                    JEANNIE
Ed, stop that.

                    SERENA
I may have been driven to the edge,
Mr. Irvine, but I'd never hurt one
of my treasured pets. You don't
believe me because you've never
experienced it. Sure, houses make
noises at night. But, after hearing
the sound of footsteps walking with
purpose throughout your house, only
to stop next to the bed you're lying
awake in, you would begin to believe
and you would fear night time as I
do.

                    JEANNIE
I'm sorry. This is new to us. We
actually had something strange
happen to us last night.

                    SERENA
Not to be rude, but I don't want to
hear about it.

                    JEANNIE
I understand. (To Edward.) You know,
if something happens here every
night, maybe we should look into it.
You know, be here when something
happens.

                    EDWARD
That's a good idea. Bring some
camcorders and audio equipment. That
would be right up Jason's alley.

                    SERENA
Why? Alyssa won't let you stay.

                    EDWARD
What makes you think so?

Just then, an OBJECT flies into view, shattering close to Edward's head. JEANNIE and EDWARD react, startled. SERENA remains calm, unfazed.

                    SERENA
          That's what makes me think so.

Edward picks up the shattered object. It is an old PHOTOGRAPH in a frame. Shattered glass from the frame lies on the floor. The photograph is of JACOB and LYDIA, with a YOUNG EDWARD standing next to them.

                    JEANNIE
          Mrs. Stevenson, let us call someone.
          Edward's brother, Jason, and his
          wife. They don't scare easily, and
          are acquainted with the whole
          situation.

                    EDWARD
          Jason helped me with the research.

                    JEANNIE
          Maybe if the entity sees we're not
          going to run away, it'll leave you
          alone.

                    EDWARD
          Or, maybe nothing will change, okay?
          But, whatever happens, we'll know
          more than we do now. And, after last
          night, we're involved already.

They wait in silence.

                    SERENA
          Alright. Do what you want. Come by
          at seven o'clock. I'll go stay with
          a friend.

                    EDWARD
          We'd better get going.

                    JEANNIE
          We'll see you tonight.

The scene fades to black, as they stand to leave.

INT. SERENA STEVENSON'S HOUSE- NIGHT

Jason and Helen are met at the front door by Edward and Jeannie.

                    EDWARD
          Hi, guys. Come inside. Welcome to the ridiculous.

                    JEANNIE
          Don't listen to him. He's just
          afraid. We had an 'incident' today,
          and he can't explain it.

                    JASON

          What happened?

                    EDWARD
          Nothing. We're wasting our time here.

Edward uses a key to let them all into the house.

                    JEANNIE
          See? Stop being so nervous. A framed
          photograph flew at us. A photograph
          of Lydia's family.

                    HELEN
          Seriously? What were you doing?

                    EDWARD
          Talking to the owner, Serena.
          According to her, that happens all
          the time.

                    JEANNIE

          And worse.

                    EDWARD
          Poltergeist activity, that's all. We
          should be looking for answers
          elsewhere.

                    JEANNIE
          Serena and I agree, it's Alyssa
          wreaking havoc on her rival's
          family. We're hoping tonight will
          provide us with answers.

The four move into the LIVING ROOM.

                    JASON

          Okay, well I brought camcorders and
          handheld voice recorders. I don't
          have all the infrared stuff the
          professionals use.

                    EDWARD
                  (Scoffing)
'Professionals'.

                    JEANNIE
Anyway, we were thinking we should
split up and each take a room. Two
down here and two upstairs.

                    HELEN
Okay, so who goes where?

                    EDWARD
Alright. Jason, you take the living
room and the front of the house.
Helen, you sit upstairs in the back
bedroom. I'll take the kitchen and
the back half of the house. Babe
(Jeannie), you watch the front
upstairs bedroom. We should each
have a sound recorder. (To
Jason.)did you bring enough?

Jason begins to unpack EQUIPMENT from a sport DUFFEL BAG.

                    JASON
Yes. Here. The green button records,
the red is for playback. I could
only get three recorders. We'll put
two downstairs and one upstairs.

                    HELEN
                  (Pleased.)
You're really getting into this.

                    JASON
I am. Things have been happening to
this family for years. I'm eager to
see it for myself.

                    JEANNIE
And I think if we can face whatever
is hassling Serena, maybe it'll
leave her and her family alone.

                    HELEN
Show it a brave front and that we're
not going to run scared.

                    EDWARD
Let's get this over with.

                          JASON
          I'll set the cameras up.

INT. SERENA'S HOUSE-LIVING ROOM- NIGHT

The scene starts with Jason and Edward having finished setting up the
cameras. The entire scene is shot only through the stationary cameras,
like 'found footage'. Each person communicates through WALKIE-TALKIES.

                          JASON
Alright. All set up.

                          EDWARD
Okay. Come on downstairs.

                          JASON
Be right down.

The scene switches to the LIVING ROOM. We see Jeannie, Edward and
Helen waiting. EDWARD enters the scene and joins them.

                          EDWARD
          Let's take our places.

                          JEANNIE
          Let's see what happens.

Everyone moves into position.

                          JASON
          Okay, I'm here.

                          HELEN
          Ready

                          JEANNIE
          All set.

                          EDWARD
          Let's do it.

                          JASON
          Here we go.

                          HELEN
                        (Giggling)
          This is so cool!

                         JEANNIE
                      (Laughing.)
          Calm down, sweetie. But, I have to
          admit, this is kinda cool. So, I
          guess we wait.

                         HELEN
          I don't know about the rest of you, but…

A PICTURE on a DRESSER next to Helen falls to the floor.

                         HELEN
          That was weird.

                         JEANNIE
          What was weird?

There is no response from Helen. A strange silence, except for some
movement from those downstairs, fills the house.

                         JEANNIE (CONT.)
          Helen?

The camera P.O.V. switches to HELEN'S ROOM. She is lying on the bed,
her eyes rolled back into her head, TREMBLING uncontrollably. She
stops trembling and lies still. We hear the others speaking through
Helen's walkie-talkie.

                         JEANNIE
          Helen?

                         JASON
          Babe? Can you hear us?

                         EDWARD
          Helen?

Helen begins to move, slowly, sluggishly.

                         HELEN
                      (Groggy.)
          I'm here. Something happened.

                         JASON
          What's wrong? What Happened?

                         JEANNIE
          I'll be right there.

                         HELEN
          No, just wait. I'm alright

                    JASON
          Okay. Everyone sit tight.

Jason's LIVING ROOM P.O.V. A small, glass BALL, sitting on a coffee
table, rolls onto the floor and breaks. We hear everyone speaking from
Jason's walkie-talkie.

                    EDWARD
          What was that?

                    JASON
          A table decoration broke. Wait. I
          hear something. Can you all feel
          that?

                    JEANNIE
          Feel what?

                    JASON
          The air. It feels thicker. Like it's
          crowding in around me.

                    EDWARD
          That's just your nerves. Relax.

Jeannie's P.O.V. The bedroom she is in is darker; the shadows are
closing in.

                    JEANNIE
          Helen, how are you doing?

                    HELEN
          I'll be alright. Ed's probably
          right. Just a nervous reaction.

                    EDWARD
          Jason, what's going on?

There is no response from Jason.

                    HELEN
          Jason? How are you doing?

From Edward's P.O.V., we hear thrashing and violent noise, items
breaking and furniture crashing, coming from Jason's area. We hear
everyone's voice from Edward's

                    EDWARD
          Jason? What's going on?

                    JASON

Oh, man. Something's here, you guys.
I think I just blacked out. The
living room's a mess.

                    Jeannie
Are you alright?

                    HELEN
Are you hurt?

                    JASON
No, just confused.

The house has taken on a decidedly darker, shadowed tone. The camera
switches from room to room. Jeannie, Edward, Jason and Helen pace
their respective area. Crawling shadows expand into each room from the
corners, closets and ceiling. The camera stops in Helen's room. From
Helen's P.O.V. she hears JEANNIE yell.

                    JEANNIE
OW!

                    HELEN
What happened?

                    JEANNIE
I agree with you guys. I think we're
only dealing with a poltergeist. A
picture flew off the wall and hit
me, just like this morning.

                    JASON
I don't know. There's a lot of damage down here.

                    EDWARD
Come on. I told you. Shit!

                    JEANNIE
Ed, what's wrong?

                    HELEN
Edward, what's wrong?

                    JASON
Ed!

From Jason's P.O.V. The house is creaking and shifting, in small,
almost imperceptible ways. A loud crash is heard from the kitchen.

                    JASON
What was that?

Everyone is silent. No-one speaks for a few seconds. More crashes are
heard from Edward's area.

                    JEANNIE
        ED!?

One by one, the DOORS in the house began to open, and then SLAM SHUT.
The slamming slowly increases in volume and speed. The sound becomes
thunderous, deafening. Beneath the sound, a high-pitched scream begins
to build.

                    HELEN
        Damn!

                    JEANNIE

        Oh, my god!

                    JASON
                 (Smiling.)
        This is so awesome.

All at once, all the doors open, then slam shut, and stop. A GROANING
SOUND, loud and low-pitched, is heard from everywhere. The HOUSE
begins to tremble, and then shake more violently.

                    JEANNIE
        Ed! (There is no answer.) Edward!!
        (No answer.) Helen! (No answer.)
        Damn it! Helen! (No answer.) Jason!
        (No answer.)

The noise continues, but becomes muted in volume. A voice speaks from
behind Jeannie. It is LYDIA, A beautiful, Spanish woman. She is angry,
pale and haggard. When speaking, her voice sounds far away.

                    LYDIA
        There is no need to shout. They
        cannot hear you.

                    JEANNIE
                 (Shocked)
        You're Lydia, I'm guessing?

                    LYDIA
        You are correct. Where is my son?

                    JEANNIE
        I have no idea where your son is?

                    LYDIA
        You Lie! I heard you calling to him, my Edward.

                    JEANNIE
        Edward is my husband.

                    LYDIA
        My son's complete name is Edward
        Andrew. Call him to join us.

Jeannie looks around her. She is no longer in Serena's home. She is in
the living room of the Stevenson mansion. It is decorated in a late
VICTORIAN manner, but everything appears old and worn out. The scenes
are shot in muted GRAY tone.

                    JEANNIE
        Where are we?

                    LYDIA
        This is my home. Mine! It does not
        belong to that pretender, Alyssa.

                    JEANNIE
        How did I get here?

                    LYDIA
        I brought you here. You are aligned
        with my son. Call him to me.

                    JEANNIE
        My husband's name is also Edward
        Andrew. But, his last name isn't
        Stevenson. It's Irvine. He was born
        decades after your son died, and is
        from a different family line.

Lydia shrieks at Jeannie. The air RIPPLES with the power of the shriek
and decades' old dirt and dust tornadoes through the air. Jeannie
COWERS.

                    LYDIA
        What you say is impossible. My son's
        absence has left me bereft. You are
        his wife. You stole him from me. His
        father's legacy is now my son's. Not
        yours and not Alyssa's. My son's.

                    JEANNIE
        My husband is not your son!

Jeannie SCREAMS at Lydia in anger. The scream increases in volume to
match Lydia's shriek. Lydia is thrown off balance, slamming through
furniture and into a wall. She stands and SHRIEKS. Jeannie is battered

by FLYING FURNITURE. The battle continues, each trading shrieks, until
the room is destroyed and both women are bloodied and dirty.

                         LYDIA
          I will have my son. Your mother will
          lose all, June.

                         JEANNIE
          I'm not June.

                         LYDIA
          You must all stop interfering with
          us. Your echoes are destroying me.

                         JEANNIE
          What do you mean?

                         LYDIA
          LEAVE US ALONE! I can take no more
          of you. Now, go and bring me my son!

The two women shriek and scream at each other. An EXPLOSION is heard
as the screen fades to black.

INT. HOSPITAL - JEANNIE'S ROOM - DAY

Jeannie is bandaged and bruised. Edward, Jason and Helen also sport
bruises and are bandaged from their encounters at the house. Helen
lies in a hospital bed. The scene is in bright contrast to the
previous few.

                         HELEN
          I'm staying here with you. Can you
          guys go home and get her some of her
          own blankets?

                         EDWARD
          Yes. (To Jeannie.) Do need anything else?

                         JEANNIE
          No, I'll only be here a couple of
          days. Before you go, we need to talk
          about what happened.

                         HELEN
          Later. You need to rest first.

                         JEANNIE
          No. I want to go over it while it's
          fresh in my mind.

                    EDWARD
Jeannie, when we found you, you said
"We were wrong. It's not her." Who
did you mean? What were we wrong
about?

                    HELEN
Ed, let her rest.

                    JASON
She's right, Ed. Jeannie needs some
sleep.

                    JEANNIE
You guys, seriously, I want to
discuss this now.

                    HELEN
Let us know if you get too tired.

                    JEANNIE
I will. We've been wrong about what
is causing all of this ghost
nonsense. It isn't Alyssa's spirit
at work. It's been Lydia the whole
time.

                    EDWARD
How do you know?

                    JEANNIE
I saw her. I talked to her. She's
confused and angry.

                    JASON
About what?

                    EDWARD
Before we get to that, you said you
saw her. What was that like?

                    JEANNIE
It was strange. (To Jason.) You
said, last night, that you felt as
if the air was getting thicker
around you. I experienced that same
feeling. It was almost as if I were
drowning. I could hardly breathe.
And, it was hot, like a furnace.
Also, there was no color to
anything. When she spoke to me, it

sounded like she was a million miles
away.

                    EDWARD
So, what did she say to you?

                    JEANNIE
Nothing she said made any sense. She
thinks you're her son, although I
think she hopes it more than thinks
it.

                    EDWARD

Huh?

                    JEANNIE
The room I saw her in was the living room
in the Stevenson mansion.

                    HELEN
Why there, of all places?

                    JEANNIE
She did some terrible things in her life.
If her soul is stuck there, in a ruined,
horrible version of the place she loved
most, it seems a fitting punishment.

                    JASON
There are cultures that believe nature
balances itself through vengeance, strange
as that sounds. If a soul commits wrongs
against others, nature makes it right.

                    EDWARD
I thought that was called 'karma'.

                    JASON
It's the same concept. The idea of balance.

                    JEANNIE
Anyway, if she's suffering there alone,
and I think she is, hearing that you share
the name of her son must make her frantic.

                    EDWARD
How does she even know my name at all?

                    JEANNIE
She said she heard me say it that night we
were fooling around in the cemetery.

                         HELEN
          And, you told her it was a co-incidence?

                         JEANNIE
          Yes, I told her. I don't think she wants
          to believe it. And, she hates me.

                         EDWARD
          Why?

                         JEANNIE
          She thinks I'm Alyssa's daughter, June.

                         EDWARD
          What?

                         JEANNIE
          That's why she attacked me; why I'm here.

                         EDWARD
          You don't resemble any photos of June
          we've seen.

                         JEANNIE
          In Lydia's state of distress, probably any
          woman you were with would look like June.
          She's despairing and wants company,
          family, and her former life. Until she
          gets it, she'll continue her attacks on
          anyone she thinks is stopping her from
          getting it.

                         EDWARD
          Did she say anything else?

                         JEANNIE
          Yes, and I think this is key to dealing
          with her. She said 'Leave us alone. Your
          echoes are killing me.'

Everyone is SILENT.

                         HELEN
          Does anyone have any ideas what that means?

                         EDWARD
          Not a clue.

                         JEANNIE
          No.

                         JASON
          Hmm. Maybe. Echoes could mean several
          things. Lydia's attacks have escalated
          since we began to research her family
          history. And all the thrown personal items
          and torn photographs at Serena's home has
          me thinking.

                         HELEN
          Yeah, well, it's going to have to wait.
          Jeannie needs rest. We'll talk about this
          later. I mean it. Come on, let's go, you
          two. I'm staying.

                         EDWARD
          Alright. Let's go, Jason.

INT. HOSPITAL - HALLWAY - A FEW MINUTES LATER

Edward and Jason are leaving Jeannie's HOSPITAL room.

                         EDWARD
          Okay. So, how do we end this?

                         JASON
          I think Lydia is pounded by noise.

                         EDWARD
          What?

                         JASON
          Look, we can agree that Lydia's spirit,
          her soul, is stuck here because she was a
          horrible person, right?

                         EDWARD
          Without a doubt.

                         JASON
          Okay. So, what do we know so far? She
          wants her son back, and she's destroying
          anything or anyone that's a reference to
          her or her family.

                         EDWARD
          Okay.

                         JASON
          This is a stretch, but what if part of
          making her atoning for her past 'misdeeds'
          involves hearing about them forever?

                         EDWARD
          Go on.

                         JASON
          Anytime someone has talked about Lydia or
          her family, written about them, read about
          them, whatever, she hears it, repeated,
          over and over.

                         EDWARD
          Oh, my god. That really would be hell.

                         JASON
          No kidding. Think about her comment to
          Jeannie, 'Stop talking about us. The
          echoes are killing me'. And, if she
          destroys anything or anyone who can cause
          more echoes, the noise that pounds her
          will stop growing.

                         EDWARD
          And, what about her thinking I'm her son?

                         JASON
          I don't know. Maybe Jeannie's right.
          Lydia's lonely.

                         EDWARD
          I want to check out the library Stevenson
          had built on his property. It was
          underground, and I'm not convinced many
          people know about it. There might be
          something there that could help us.

                         JASON
          I'm in. We should probably go during the
          day. Less chance of running into her
          ghost.

                         EDWARD
          Alright. Jeannie and I located it on a map
          of the grounds. Let's go. I'll stop and
          get some flashlights on the way.

                         JASON
          Cool.

EXT. STEVENSON OUTDOOR GROUNDS-DAY

Edward and Jason search for the entrance to the
library.

                         JASON
          What makes you think we'll even be able to
          get into the library, if we find it?

                         EDWARD
          Lydia loves me, remember? She'll make sure
          we get inside. This is just about where
          the old library showed up on the map. Keep
          your eyes open.

They search through the trees and bushes for a few minutes. Edward
STUMBLES and falls.

                         EDWARD
          Dammit!

                         JASON
                      (Laughing.)
          Are you okay?

                         EDWARD
          Yeah., I'm alright. Come here. There's a
          trapdoor.

                         JASON
          Awesome.

They stare at an old TRAPDOOR set into the ground.

                         EDWARD
          Well, let's find out what's down there.

                         JASON
          Cool.

They both remove flashlights. Edward wrenches open the trapdoor. They
both react to a BAD SMELL.

                         JASON
          After you.

Edward climbs downstairs out of sight. Jason follows him.

INT. STEVENSON MANSION - UNDERGROUND LIBRARY - DAY

Edward and Jason walk down steps into a LARGE, DARK ROOM. Old
bookshelves line the walls, covered by dusty, worm-eaten TOMES, some
very old. In one corner is a BED, with leather straps attached to it.
In one wall is a HIDDEN door, leading through a TUNNEL, to the mansion
living room.

                         JASON
          Damn, this is fantastic.

                         EDWARD
          It's a dump. C'mon, let's look around and get out of here.

                         JASON
          Buddy, you need a stronger sense of adventure.

                         EDWARD
          All I need is my television.

They search the BOOKSHELVES, examining the books. They also examine
the bed.

                         JASON
          Here's something. Check this out.

Jason hands Edward a leather-bound JOURNAL.

                         EDWARD
          It's a diary. The cover says 'MY MEMOIRS:
          JACOB STEVENSON'. I guess the old man
          wanted to document his crimes for
          prosperity.

Edward hands the journal back to Jason, who thumbs through it.

                         JASON
          If you can believe this, he was a hero,
          gave a lot of money to charity, endured
          unfair slander and gossip and was unjustly
          accused of crimes he didn't commit.

                         EDWARD
          (Looking at the straps attached to the
          bed.) Yeah, he was a real saint. What else
          does it tell?

Pages from the journal APPEAR and FADE from the screen as Jason
relates what is written in it.

                         JASON
          Well, it says his business in textiles was
          doing very well. His marriage to Alyssa
          was pleasant to him. He does mention her
          child. She had a difficult birth. And here
          it is. He writes about his disappointment
          that she gave birth to a girl. Hmm.

                                EDWARD
          What? Let me see. According to this,
          Joseph was planning to take care of the
          child. It looks like he actually cared
          about her. Look at this. The handwriting
          changes from a strong script to a weak and
          shaky hand.

                                JASON
          And, there's Lydia's name. The tone of his
          entries turns really dark. His business is
          failing…the community is turning against
          him…He fears for his daughter's safety.
          And look. The script, towards the end,
          changes to what looks like a woman's
          handwriting. My god.

Edward reads over Jason's shoulder.

                                EDWARD
          Damn. She was one vengeful bitch! She
          wanted the old man's money, and the son as
          his heir, and it didn't matter to her how
          she did it.

                                JASON
          The last entry is 'he made his bed, now he's lying under it.'

Both men look in shock at the old bed with the LEATHER STRAPS.

                             EDWARD/JASON
          Damn!

Both men move to the bed, grab a hold of it, and pull it away from the
wall. Hidden by the bed is Jacob Stevenson's SKELETON, A burn mark is
visible on his forehead. The coat and vest of his old suit are
scorched. They kneel down to examine the body.

                                JASON
          It almost looks like he was struck in the
          head with a lightning bolt.

                                EDWARD
          See what's in his pockets.

                                JASON
          No, you do it.

                                EDWARD
          Alright

As soon as Edward touches the skeleton, the room begins to shake, as if in an earthquake. The hidden door slowly opens, spewing dirt and dust. Both men walk towards it. From far down the corridor beyond, a piercing shriek is heard. The men stop at the door.

                    JASON
          You're kidding? This is incredible.

                    EDWARD
          Maybe you need less of a sense of adventure.

Another shriek is heard.

                    EDWARD
          I suppose we'd better check that out.

Suddenly, the room quakes again. With a yell, Edward is yanked into the dark corridor. Jason is horrified. As he looks around, from a distance, we hear Edward scream in pain. Lydia shrieks again. Jason runs through the corridor, and comes out into the Stevenson living room, but it is the gray, dinghy, dilapidated version That Jeannie saw. Jason's movements are in slow motion as soon as he enters the scene. He hears shrieks and screams from the second floor. He races up the stairs (in slow motion) to the second floor. Edward lies unconscious. Jason kneels, and then turns to look over his shoulder, reacting in shock. Lydia stands glaring at him. She shrieks, sending Jason into a nearby wall. He drops to the floor unconscious. The scene fades to black.

INT. STEVENSON MANSION/SECOND FLOOR-DAY

Edward regains consciousness. Sitting up, in obvious pain, he looks around. Light filters through dusty windows to show a dinghy, empty mansion.

                    EDWARD
          Jason! Jason, where are you!

He hears movement behind him. Turning quickly, he sees Jason regaining consciousness.

                    EDWARD
          Are you alright?

Jason holds his arm.

                    JASON
          No. My arm's broken.

Edward stands and helps Jason to his feet.

                    EDWARD
         We've been here several hours. You can
         tell, it's light outside. We need to get
         to a hospital.

They limp downstairs and open the front door. They walk outside, the
camera zooming in on them.

                    EDWARD/JASON
         Damn.

Parked in front of the house are two POLICE CRUISERS. Jeannie and
Helen stand next to police officers, who beckon to the men. The scene
fades to black.

INT. EDWARD and JEANNIE'S HOUSE - TWO MOTHS LATER - DUSK

Edward and Jeannie are exhausted and careworn. The house is no longer
clean and tidy. Throughout the following scene, the house ROCKS and
SHAKES, as in an earthquake, and a distant WAILING is heard. Edward is
on the phone to Jason.

                    EDWARD
         Jason, would you just call them for us?
         We're at our wits end. Nothing else has
         worked. No, he isn't returning our calls.
         Not since he left before he could bless
         the house. No, Jason. We can't find anyone
         else, and Lydia is ignoring our pleas. How
         much do they want to help us? Geezus!
         Alright, see if they can come here today.
         Talk to you later.

                    JEANNIE
         How much do they want?

                    EDWARD
         Five thousand dollars. Can you believe it?

                    JEANNIE
         I don't care, Ed. I want her out of our
         lives. We have been dealing with this long
         enough, and I want it to STOP! Give them
         their damn money. When are they getting
         here?

                    EDWARD
         Jason said they should be here soon. They
         were on a job nearby yesterday.

                    JEANNIE
         What did he find out about them?

                              EDWARD
            They've been working together for a while.
            They're expensive, and they get results.

                              JEANNIE
            I'm going to lie down for a while. Let me
            know when they get here.

Jeannie lies down on the COUCH, while Edward thumbs through a
newspaper. The scene interchanges between Edward and Jeanne, each
reacting to various frightening noises and tremblings in the house.
Finally, a knock is heard on the front door.

                              EDWARD
            Jeannie! I think it's them.

                              JEANNIE
            Finally!

They open the front door to two men. Their names are DES RIKER and
CULL COWEN. Each is tough and dressed as a biker, i.e. leather vest,
long hair, boots.

                              DES
            Hello. Are you the Irvines?

                              EDWARD
            Yes, we are.

                              DEC
            Your brother, Jason, called us. He said
            you needed our help.

                              EDWARD
            Yes, we do. What are your names?

                              DES
            I'm Des Riker. This is Cull Cowen. We just
            finished a job over on Saint Invictus
            Street. A frightened spirit that didn't
            want to leave his mama. (Both men laugh.)

                              JEANNIE
            Frightened?

                              DES
            Yeah, believe it or not. They have…

A piercing shriek is heard. At the same time, the house shakes. Des
and Cullen exchange a look, and then smile.

                              DES
         May we come in?

The Irvines step aside to admit Des and Cull into their home, closing
the door behind them.

                              EDWARD
         Let's go out onto the back porch. There's
         a table there. It'll be quieter.

Another shriek is heard. All four walk through the living room, and
exit through the back door. They stand on the porch. EVENING is
falling.

                              DES
         I think we should start right away.

                              JEANNIE
         It's too late to get to a bank. We can get
         it first thing tomorrow. Five thousand
         dollars, right?

                              DES
         Yeah, five thousand. But, don't worry, we
         don't ask for payment until the thing is
         completely out of your lives.

                              EDWARD
         So, where do we do this? Here at the house?

                              DES
         I wouldn't recommend it. These situations
         can get messy. Best if it's done off the
         property.

                              JEANNIE
         That should be easy. She goes with us
         everywhere. The grocery store, a
         restaurant, it doesn't matter.

                              DES
         You said 'she'?

                              EDWARD
         Did Jason give you any information about
         what's going on?

                              DES
         He gave us a rundown. He mentioned a man
         and some woman. And a couple of children.

                              EDWARD

It's one of those women who are doing
this. She thinks I'm her son.

                    DES
          Your brother mentioned echoes. They make
          things worse. Your spirit lady is probably
          ready to tear the world apart.

                    JEANNIE
          She's already started. Have you seen our
          house? We've been saying nice things about
          her family and apologizing for everything,
          but its only gotten worse.

                    DES
          I'm sure it has. We need to move fast. Is
          there somewhere else we can lure her to?

                    EDWARD
          Stevenson mansion. It's not that far from
          here. It's where everything started.

                    DES
          Okay. We'll meet you there.

INT. STEVENSON MANSION- NIGHT

Edward, Jeannie, Des and Cull enter the mansion, breaking into a side
door.

                    EDWARD
          Okay, the living room is through there.

                    JEANNIE
          Lydia brought me there the first time she
          attacked us.

                    DES
          Alright, then. We'll confront her in the
          living room.

Des and Cull open a DUFFEL BAG and Des takes out a BASEBALL BAT with
spikes, while Cull removes an AXE.

                    EDWARD
          Whoa! You came prepared.

                    DES
          We always do.

                    JEANNIE
          How do those things work against ghosts?

                         DES
          They're coated with the blood of Aztec
          sacrificial victims, and tipped with
          silver from pre-Columbian spirit chalices.

                         EDWARD
          Are you serious?

                         DES
          Nah. We just cover them with holy water.

Cull laughs and takes out a HIP-FLASK with a cross engraved on it, and
filled with HOLY WATER. He pours some on each weapon, and then
sprinkles some on each person.

                         EDWARD
          Uh, thanks. Does that help?

                         CULL
          Couldn't hurt.

                         JEANNIE
          You do actually speak.

                         CULL
          Not much.

                         DES
          Now, we're going to call the ghost.

                         JEANNIE
          Lydia.

                         DES
          Right, Lydia. We're going to call Lydia to
          us. We can't let her leave this place, if
          we're going to stop her.

Cull takes a three-foot-tall CANDLE out of the duffel, sets it down,
and lights it.

                         EDWARD
          Is that from the 'Aztecs' too?

                         DES
          Something like that.

                         JEANNIE
          Do we need to draw a pentagram or
          anything? A circle of protection,
          something like that?

                              DES
          If it will make you feel better. But, in
          our experience, nothing like that ever
          helps.

                            EDWARD
          How does holy water help?

                              DES
          I don't know. We've tried all kinds of
          weapons and concoctions people have
          suggested, but blessed water is the only
          thing that acts as a deterrent. And I'm
          not even religious. I just know it works.

                            JEANNIE
                           (Sincere.)
          That's good to hear.

                            EDWARD
                          (Sarcastic)
          Terrific

                              DES
          Alright. Start calling her name. Let's go.

                            EDWARD
          Here, I brought this. (Edward takes a
          PHOTOGRAPH from his pocket.)I took it from
          a woman we met (to Jeannie)…Serena…(to
          Des) who was also plagued by the ghost. It
          shows Lydia and her family.

Des and Cull look at the photograph, then Des drops the photo on the
floor and Cull destroys it with his axe.

                              DES
          I'm sorry, but we can't mess around. That
          should get her attention.

With an explosion of SOUND and ENERGY, everyone is SLAMMED against the
walls.

                            EDWARD
          I think she's here.

The air ripples with energy. The scene turns to muted grays. In the
center of the room, LYDIA appears, furious and shrieking. Everyone
stands to face her. Des and Cull heft their weapons and moves towards
her. Lydia turns to face Edward.

                              LYDIA
        My son. Where have you been? I'm desolate without you. Our home
        is cold and drear in your absence.

Cull walks up behind Lydia and hits her with the ax. She reacts with a
startled look of pain, and then emits a shriek which throws him
against a wall. Des then approaches Lydia and hits her with his spiked
bat. Again, she reacts and shrieks, slamming Des to the ground. She
turns to Edward.

                              LYDIA
        You see, my son? I am battered and beaten. Please, help me.

Again, Des and Cull assault Lydia, who reacts with pain, shrieking to
repel them.

                              LYDIA
        Edward! Please help me!

Again, Des and Cull ATTACK. Same reaction from Lydia.

                             EDWARD
        Lydia! I am not your son! You're mistaken!

                             JEANNIE
                            (Horrified)
        Oh, god. Edward, no!

                               DES
        Don't tell her that. Are you crazy?

                             EDWARD
        No. I've had enough. Lydia, I'm not your
        son. Yes, my name is Edward. And my middle
        name is Andrew. It's only a coincidence.
        My wife's name is Jeannie. She isn't
        Alyssa's daughter, June.

Lydia turns to GLARE at Jeannie. Des and Cull attack Lydia again. She
reacts in pain, but does not shriek. She turns to face Edward again.

                             JEANNIE
        Edward, stop. She's not going to understand.

                              LYDIA
        Silence, whelp. Do not speak to my son again.

Lydia shrieks again, sending Jeannie against a wall.

                              EDWARD
          Lydia. That's enough. We're sorry for your
          suffering. But, you have to stop. I
          promise you, I'm not your son.

Des and Cull brace themselves.

                              DES
          Here it comes. Everyone brace yourselves!

As Lydia shrieks in frustration and despair, the house shakes and the
air ripples. The intensity grows.

                              JACOB
          Lydia!

JACOB STEVENSON appears, angry at Lydia and generating his own energy.

                              JACOB
          Release these people immediately.

Lydia faces Jacob. During the following EXCHANGE, Edward, Jeannie, Des
and Cull stare in shock and fascination. The air Thunders and vibrates
with the energy of the ghostly confrontation.

                              LYDIA
          You! This is your fault. You should have
          given me all. It was my right, as your
          wife.

                              JACOB
          You are nothing more than an angry witch!
          You destroyed my first wife, Alyssa. You
          destroyed my reputation, and then tortured
          and killed me. Even your son did not love
          you. Are you aware that he was the one who
          caused your death?

                              Lydia
          You wretched bastard. How dare you say
          that? My son adored me.

                              JACOB
          You delude yourself. Your son hated you.
          He married June so you would get nothing.

                              LYDIA
          You lie! I could have had it all. I was
          your love. I should have had it all. And
          now, everyone will pay!

Jacob and Lydia begin to BATTLE, their various energies blasting one
another. In the midst of their fight, Edward, Jeannie, Des and Cull
watch FASCINATED. The house shakes and begins to CRUMBLE. Des SHOUTS
to be heard over the noise.

                         Des
              We should get the hell out! Now!

The four BOLT from the room. They exit the house through the front
door. Through the windows, we see FLASHES OF LIGHT. The ground outside
trembles. As the four run onto the front yard, a MASSIVE EXPLOSION
tears the house apart and flings Edward, Jeannie, Des and Cull to the
ground. They stand and brush themselves off.

                         JEANNIE
              Do you think she's gone?

                         DES
              In our experience, something that loud and
              explosive means it's over.

                         EDWARD
              Never seen anything like it. Well, you can
              crash at the house tonight, and I'll get
              you your money tomorrow.

                         DES
              Nah. We'll go home and come to your house
              tomorrow. And, since we didn't rid you of
              Lydia's spirit, you only owe us a grand.

                         EDWARD
              Okay, thanks. And, we appreciate your
              help. I gotta be honest, I didn't think
              you were legitimate. But, you definitely
              did your part.

                         DES
              You're welcome.

They all shake hands.

                         DES
              Come on, Cull. Let's go. Good night.

                         EDWARD
              Good night. See you tomorrow.

                         JEANNIE
              Thank you.

INT. EDWARD/JEANNIE'S HOME- NIGHT

Edward, Jeannie, Jason and Helen sit around the kitchen table. All are visibly more relaxed. They sip wine and coffee.

                    JEANNIE
          …and so, we actually got a full, quiet
          night's sleep last night.

                    EDWARD
          Whatever happened inside the mansion after
          we fled, it worked. All yesterday and
          today we spent cleaning up around the
          house.

                    JEANNIE
          And I took time to paint.

                    HELEN
          That's wonderful.

                    JASON
          Have you spoken to Serena yet, to see how
          she's doing?

                    JEANNIE
          We called her today. She cried the whole
          conversation. It was a quiet night for her
          too, her first in ages. She asked us to
          tell you 'thank you' as well.

                    HELEN
          What about these two 'ghost bashers' you
          hired?

                    EDWARD
          They were honest. A complete surprise to
          both of us. They waded right in and stood
          up to Lydia. Personally, I was prepared
          for them to be a complete scam, but they
          weren't.

                    JEANNIE
          And they gave us a break on the price,
          because it was actually Jacob Stevenson
          who got rid of her.

                    HELEN
          Yeah, about that…

                    EDWARD
          Unfortunately, we didn't stick around to
          watch their final argument. But, the old

man actually stood up against her for us.
Maybe the stories about him being a
bastard were incorrect.

                    JASON
That final confrontation must have been
something to see. The emergency services
were busy for four hours putting out the
blaze.

                    HELEN
That's fine. Let Jacob and Lydia scream at
each other for eternity.

                    JASON
Maybe.

                    EDWARD
What?

                    JASON
Well, with Jacob showing up like he did, I
hope it didn't leave any doors open for
him, or anyone else, to return.

                    JEANNIE
No. No, I'm not listening to that. They're
gone. Period.

                    HELEN
You're right, Jeannie. They're gone. (To
Jason.) Come on, you. It's late. Let's go
home.

They all stand, as the scene FADES. The credits begin to roll, as the
camera pans through the DARKENED house. The credits end at an open
window, the curtains billowing. The camera zooms onto JACON STEVENSON
staring through the window, into the house.

Fade out